U0930240

快速发展的中国高速铁路

The Rapid Development of China's High-Speed Railways

中国国家铁路集团有限公司
CHINA STATE RAILWAY GROUP CO., LTD.

中国铁道出版社有限公司
CHINA RAILWAY PUBLISHING HOUSE CO., LTD.
2019年 · 北　京
2019 · Beijing

前 言

中国政府高度重视高速铁路的发展，经过多年的技术研究、工程实践和安全运营，高铁事业取得举世瞩目的巨大成就。目前，中国投入运营的高速铁路突破2.9万公里，“四纵四横”高铁网提前建成运营，“八纵八横”高铁网建设全面展开。

中国是世界上高速铁路运营里程最长、在建规模最大、商业运营速度最高、高铁技术最全面、运营场景和管理经验最为丰富的国家。

编印《快速发展的中国高速铁路》一书，旨在从中国高速铁路概况、发展历程、关键技术、主要特点、为人民创造的美好生活、未来发展方向和规划目标等方面，介绍中国高速铁路发展情况，希望能够帮助大家更好地了解中国高速铁路。

Preface

The Chinese government attaches great important to the high-speed railway (HSR) development. After years of technological research, engineering practice and safe operation, great achievements in high-speed railway industry attracted world attention. Today China's HSR mileage in operation has exceeded 29,000 km. Four horizontal and four vertical national railway network started operation ahead of schedule. Moreover, the construction of eight horizontal and eight vertical national railway network has fully launched.

China now has the longest HSR mileage both in operation and under construction, the highest business operation speed, the most complete technologies, the vastest variety of operation scenarios and management experiences in the world.

The Rapid Development of China's HSRs gives a general picture about HSR development in China, from aspects such as overview, history, key technologies, main features, contributions to social and economic development, as well as future development trend and goals, so as to give readers a better understanding of HSRs in China.

快速发展的中国高速铁路

The Rapid Development of China's High-Speed Railways

⊙北京南站开出的复兴号高速列车
Fuxing High-Speed Train Departs from Beijingnan Railway Station

目 录

Contents

第 1 章 中国高速铁路概况

Chapter 1 Overview

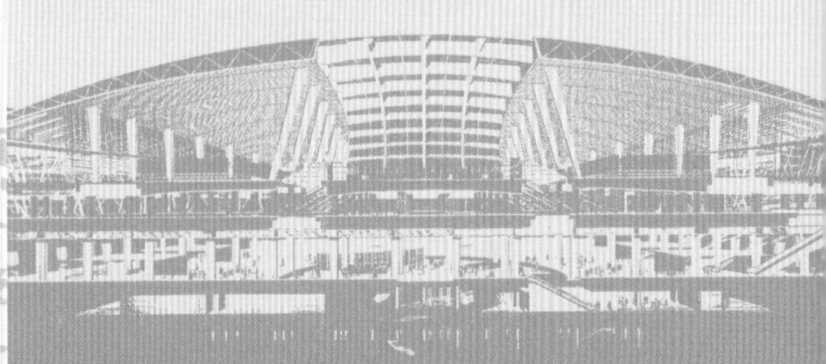

高速铁路具有安全可靠、方便快捷、运力强大、节能环保等优势。中国幅员辽阔、人口众多，正处于工业化、城镇化深入发展时期，发展高速铁路意义重大，正逢其时。

HSR has many advantages such as safe, reliable, convenient, fast, powerful, energy-efficient and environment-friendly. China has a vast territory , a large population and now is undergoing deepening process of industrialization and urbanization, hence the development of HSR bears great significance and comes at just the right time.

经过多年的探索实践，中国高速铁路发展速度快、建设规模大、运输能力强，高铁技术水平总体迈入世界先进行列，部分领域达到世界领先水平。近年来，按照国家《中长期铁路网规划》和“十一五”“十二五”“十三五”规划，中国加快推进高速铁路建设，“四纵四横”高铁网提前建成运营。到2018年底，中国高速铁路营业里程突破2.9万公里，占世界高铁总里程的三分之二以上，是世界上高速铁路运营里程最长、在建规模最大、商业运营速度最高、高铁技术最全面、运营场景和管理

Through years of research and practice, China's HSR has become a leader in this area owing to the rapid development pace, large scale construction and huge transport capacity, with the overall technologies among the most advanced technologies in the world and some even leading the world. In recent years, according to the ***Medium and Long Term Railway Network Program*** and the 11th, 12th and 13th Five-year Plans, China has dedicated more efforts to HSR construction. The HSR network undergirded by "four horizontal and four vertical "national railway network has entered service ahead of the plan. By the end of 2018, China's HSR mileage in operation had exceeded 29,000 km, accounting for more than 66.3% of the total in the world. China now has the longest HSR mileage both in operation and under

⊙京沪高速铁路北京南至廊坊间
Beijing-Shanghai High-Speed Railway (Beijingnan-Langfang)

复兴号

经验最为丰富的国家。

快速发展的中国高速铁路，正在改变着中国人的出行方式。截至2018年底，动车组列车累计发送旅客96亿人次，占铁路旅客发送量的比重由2007年的4.5%增长到62.5%。

⊙京沪高速铁路淮河特大桥
Beijing-Shanghai High-Speed Railway (Huai River Bridge)

construction, the highest business operation speed, the most complete technologies, the vastest variety of operation scenarios and management experiences in the world.

The rapid HSR development in China is now changing the way people travel. By the end of 2018, the total number of passengers carried by EMU trains reached 9.6 billion, and the share of passengers carried by EMU (Electrical Multiple Unit) in total railway passengers increased from 4.5% in 2007 to 62.5%.

中长期高速铁路网规划图

Medium and Long Term High-Speed Railway Network Program

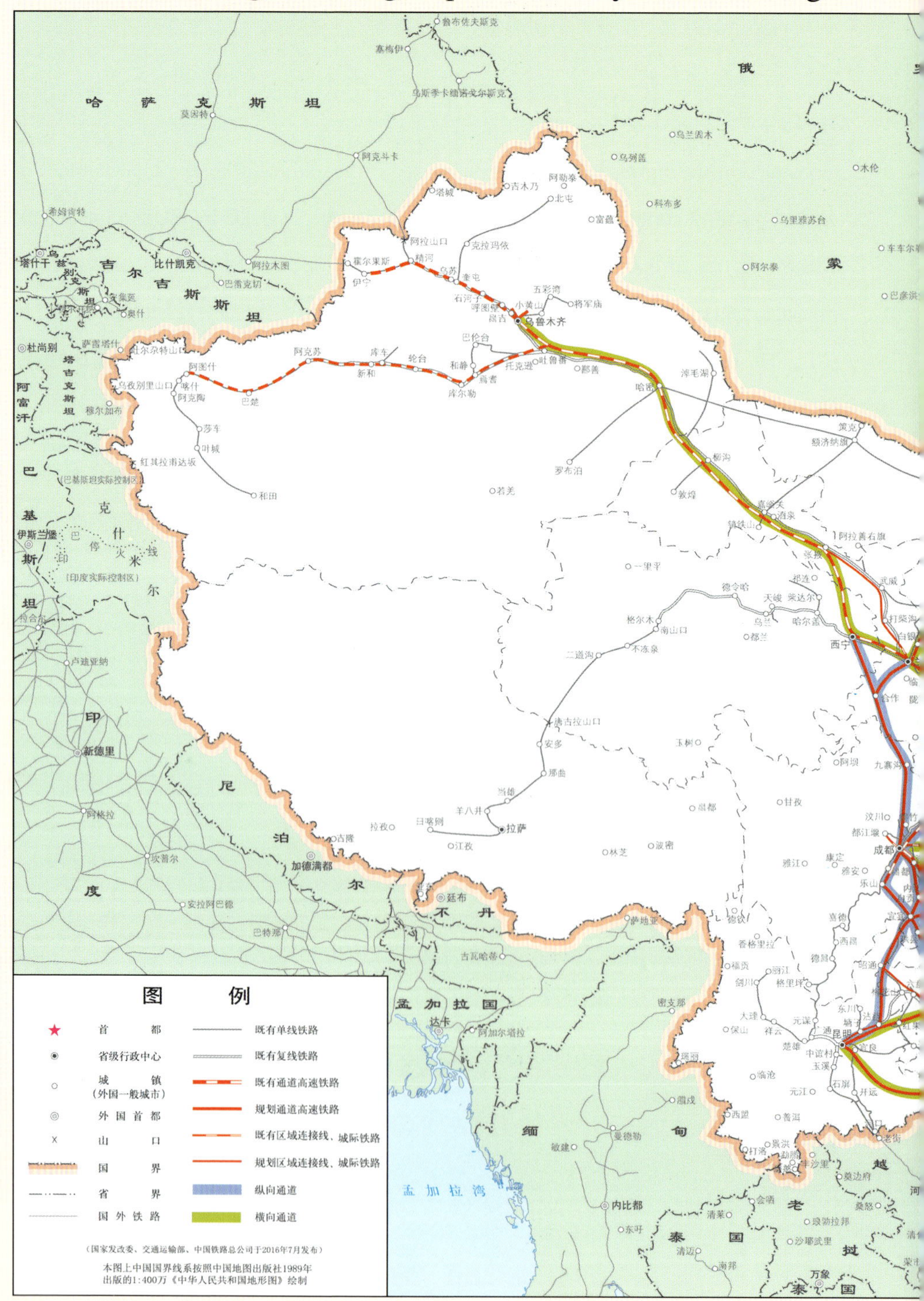

图审字：GS（2019）2710号

第 2 章
中国高速铁路发展历程
Chapter 2 History

上个世纪九十年代，中国开始在高速铁路领域进行研究探索，在较短的时间内取得了重大进步，高速铁路技术实现重大突破，高速铁路建设和运营规模迅速跃居世界首位。

China has started the HSR research and development (R&D) since the 1990s and achieved significant progress in a short period of time with major breakthroughs. Both the construction and operation scale are now ranking the first in the world.

1994年12月22日，全长147公里、由原广州至深圳铁路改建而成的广州至深圳准高速铁路投入运营，最高运营时速达到160公里。

1997年至2007年，中国铁路完成六次既有线大提速，繁忙干线提速区段最高运营时速达到200公里。

2003年10月12日，全长405公里、新建的秦皇岛至沈阳客运专线投入运营，最高运营时速达到200公里，为高速铁路建设进行了一定的技术准备。

2004年1月，中国政府发布了《中长期铁路网规划》，提出规划建设"四纵四横"铁路快速客运通道，其中客运专线1.2万

The Guangzhou-Shenzhen quasi-high-speed railway with a total length of 147 km, which was reconstructed from the original Guangzhou-Shenzhen Railway, was put into operation on December 22, 1994, with a maximum operating speed of 160 km/h.

China Railway completed six large-scale speed-up of existing lines from 1997 to 2007, and the maximum operating speed of the busy trunk line speed-up section reached 200 kilometers per hour.

The 405 km new Passenger-Dedicated Line (PDL) from Qinhuangdao to Shenyang entered operation on October 12, 2003, with a maximum operating speed of 200 km per hour, which made certain technical preparations for the construction of high-speed railway.

In January 2004, the ***Medium and Long Term Railway Network Program*** issued by Chinese Government proposed to

⊙秦沈客运专线线路
Qinhuangdao-Shenyang PDL

0087
0088

公里以上。

2008年8月1日，我国第一条设计时速350公里，全长118公里，穿越松软土地区的北京至天津城际高速铁路开通运营。

build the four horizontal and four vertical national railway network, including over 12,000 km passenger-dedicated lines.

The 118 km Beijing-Tianjin intercity HSR opened crossing over soft and loose soil area on August 1, 2008, which is the first HSR with design speed of 350 km per hour in China.

⊙北京至天津城际高速铁路
Beijing-Tianjin Intercity High-Speed Railway

⊙天津站
Tianjin Railway Station

○北京南站
Beijingnan Railway Station

2008年10月，中国政府发布了《中长期铁路网规划（调整）》，提出建设客运专线1.6万公里。

2010年2月6日，全长553公里，世界上首条修建在大面积湿陷性黄土地区的郑州至西安高速铁路开通运营。

In October 2008, Chinese Government issued the revised the ***Medium and Long Term Railway Network Program***, proposing to build 16,000 km passenger-dedicated lines.

The 553 km Zhengzhou-Xi'an HSR opened on February 6 , 2010, as the world's first HSR built on large collapsible loess areas.

⊙郑州东站
Zhengzhoudong Railway Station

ZHENGZHOU EAST RAILWAY STATION

⊙ 郑州东站进出站通道
Entering and Leaving Passage of Zhengzhoudong Railway Station

⊙郑州至西安高速铁路
Zhengzhou-Xi'an High-Speed Railway

⊙西安北站
Xi'anbei Railway Station

⊙西安北站内景
In Xi'anbei Railway Station

2010年7月1日，全长323公里，贯穿中国最密集城市群的上海至南京城际高速铁路开通运营。

The 323 km Shanghai-Nanjing intercity HSR opened on July 1, 2010, crossing the most densely populated region in China.

⊙上海至南京城际高速铁路昆山南站
Shanghai-Nanjing Intercity High-Speed Railway (Kunshannan Railway Station)

⊙上海至南京高速铁路
Shanghai-Nanjing High-Speed Railway

⊙南京南站
Nanjingnan Railway Station

⊙上海虹桥站
Shanghai Hongqiao Railway Station

2011年6月30日，当今世界速度标准最高，运营列车试验速度最高（时速达486.1公里），全长1318公里的北京至上海高速铁路开通运营。

The 1,318 km Beijing-Shanghai HSR opened on June 30, 2011, creating a highest testing speed record (486.1 km/h) in the world. It's the world's highest speed standard.

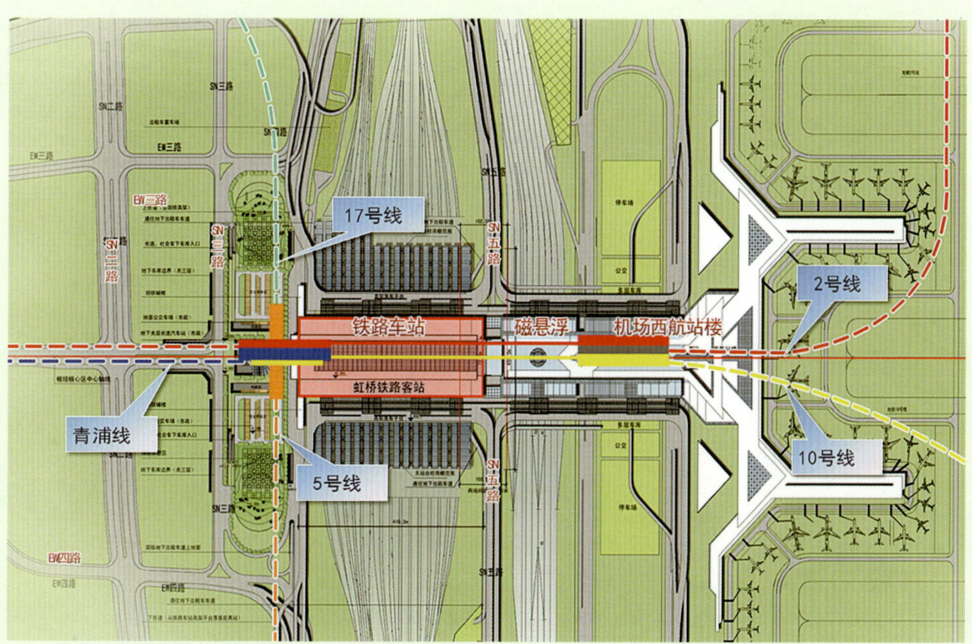

⊙上海虹桥站总平面图
General Layout of Shanghai Hongqiao Railway Station

◎京沪高速铁路跨越阳澄湖的丹阳至昆山特大桥
Beijing-Shanghai High-Speed Railway (Danyang-Kunshan)

2012年12月1日，全长921公里，世界上第一条穿越高寒季节性冻土地区的哈尔滨至大连高速铁路开通运营。

The 921 km Ha'erbin-Dalian HSR opened on December 1, 2012, as the first HSR crossing permafrost area in the world.

⊙哈尔滨至大连高速铁路
Ha'erbin-Dalian High-Speed Railway

⊙哈尔滨西站
Ha'erbinxi Station

⊙大连北站
Dalianbei Railway Station

2012年12月26日，全长2281公里，世界上运营里程最长、跨越温带亚热带、多种地形地质区域和众多水系的北京至广州高速铁路全线通车。

The 2,281 km Beijing-Guangzhou HSR opened on December 26, 2012, as the longest HSR in the world, running through temperate and subtropical zones with different topographical and geological features and many river systems.

⊙北京西站
Beijingxi Railway Station

⊙广州南站
Guangzhounan Railway Station

2013年12月28日，全长1464公里，连接长江三角洲、海峡西岸和珠江三角洲的杭州至宁波至深圳的东南沿海高速铁路全线贯通运营。

The 1,464 km southeast coastal HSR opened on December 28, 2013, connecting the Yangtze River Delta, the west coast of Taiwan Straits and the Pearl River Delta Region.

⊙杭州东站
Hangzhoudong Railway Station

⊙北京至广州高速铁路
Beijing-Guangzhou High-Speed Railway

2014年12月26日，全长1785公里，世界上一次建成里程最长、穿越戈壁沙漠地带和大风区的兰州至乌鲁木齐高速铁路开通运营。

The 1,785 km Lanzhou-Urumqi HSR opened on December 26, 2014, as the longest HSR built in one phase in the world, running through the Gobi Desert zone and windy regions.

⊙兰州西站
Lanzhouxi Railway Station

⊙兰州至乌鲁木齐高速铁路
Lanzhou-Urumqi High-Speed Railway

⊙乌鲁木齐站
Urumqi Railway Station

2015年6月28日，全长850公里，合肥至福州高速铁路开通运营。

2015年12月30日，全长653公里，世界上首条穿越热带滨海地区的环岛高铁——海南环岛高速铁路开通运营。

The 850 km Hefei-Fuzhou HSR opened on June 28.

The 653 km Hainan Island High-Speed Loop Line Railway opened on December 30, 2015, as the first Loop Line Railway crossing tropical coastal areas in the world.

⊙合肥南站
Hefeinan Railway Station

⊙福州站
Fuzhou Railway Station

⊙合肥至福州高速铁路
Hefei-Fuzhou High-Speed Railway

⊙海南环岛高速铁路神州至陵水间
Hainan Island High-Speed Loop Line Railway (Shenzhou-Lingshui)

⊙海南环岛高速铁路琼海至博鳌间
Hainan Island High-Speed Loop Line Railway (Qionghai-Bo'ao)

2016年7月，中国政府发布了新的《中长期铁路网规划》，提出规划建设“八纵八横”高速铁路网。

2016年7月15日，中国自行设计研制、拥有自主知识产权的中国标准动车组，在郑州至徐州高速铁路进行的综合试验中，成功实现时速420公里交会和重联运行。这一试验在世界高铁运营列车尚属首次。

⊙中国标准动车组在郑徐高铁实现时速420公里交会和重联运行

In July 2016, Chinese government published the updated ***Medium and Long Term Railway Network Program***, which proposed to build a HSR network with eight vertical and eight horizontal trunk lines.

On July 15, 2016, during a comprehensive test on the Zhengzhou-Xuzhou HSR, two Chinese Standard EMUs, which are independently developed by China with Intellectual Property Protection (IPR), passed each other in opposite directions on parallel tracks at a speed of 420 km/h. This test is the first time in the world for high-speed train operation.

Meeting and coupled operation of China standard EMUs at 420 km/h on Zhengzhou-Xuzhou HSR

2016年12月28日，全长2252公里，横贯东西、经过省份最多的上海至昆明高速铁路全线开通。

The 2,252 km Shanghai-Kunming HSR, the longest horizontal HSR in China crossing the largest number of provinces, was put into full operation on December 28, 2016.

⊙昆明南站
Kunmingnan Railway Station

⊙上海至昆明高速铁路
Shanghai-Kunming High-Speed Railway

2017年9月21日，复兴号中国标准动车组按时速350公里在北京至上海高速铁路商业运营，树立了世界高铁建设运营新标杆。

The Fuxing EMUs was introduced in regular service between Beijing and Shanghai at a speed of 350 km/h on September 21, 2017, setting a new benchmark for HSR operation in the world.

⊙复兴号动车组实现时速350公里运行
Fuxing EMUs Achieve 350 km/h

2017年12月6日，全长658公里，中国首条穿越地理和气候南北分界线——秦岭的西安至成都高速铁路开通运营，破解“蜀道难”取得历史性突破。

The 658 km Xi'an-Chengdu HSR opened on December 6, 2017, as the first HSR in China, running through the Qinling Mountains, the geographical and climate boundary between north and south of China. This line achieves a historical breakthrough.

⊙西成高速铁路新场街站

Xi'an-Chengdu High-Speed Railway (Xinchangjie Railway Station)

⊙西成高速铁路

Xi'an-Chengdu High-Speed Railway

2018年9月23日，全长141公里，连接香港和内地的广州至深圳至香港高速铁路全线开通运营，香港进入全国高速铁路网。

The 141 km Guangzhou-Shenzhen-Hong Kong HSR opened on September 23, 2018, connecting Hong Kong, Guangzhou and Shenzhen . Hong Kong is accessed to the national HSR network.

⊙旅客在香港西九龙站候车
The Waiting Room in West Kowloon Terminus

⊙旅客乘广深港高铁抵达香港

Passengers Arrive in Hong Kong by the Guangzhou-Shenzhen-Hong Kong High-Speed Railway

⊙旅客与动感号列车合影留念

Passengers Take Pictures with High-Speed Train

⊙广深港高铁西九龙站外景
West Kowloon Terminus

2018年12月25日，全长272公里，绿色生态黄金旅游线杭州至黄山高速铁路开通运营。

The 272 km Hangzhou-Mount Huang HSR opened on December 25, 2018, crossing many popular green eco-tourism destinations.

⊙杭黄高速铁路千岛湖站
Hangzhou-Mount Huang High-Speed Railway (Qiandaohu Railway Station)

第3章 中国高速铁路关键技术

Chapter 3 Key HSR Technologies

经过多年的科学研究和工程实践，中国构建了完备的高速铁路技术体系，覆盖勘察设计、工程建造、高速列车、牵引供电、运营管理、安全保障等各个方面，总体技术水平迈入世界先进行列，部分领域达到世界领先水平，复兴号高速列车迈出从追赶到领跑的关键一步。

With years of R&D and engineering practice, a complete Chinese HSR technology system has been established covering HSR survey & design, engineering & construction, high-speed EMU trains, traction power supply, operation management, safety and security, etc. The overall HSR technologies are among the most advanced technologies in the world, with some of them being the cutting-edge technologies. Fuxing HSR has taken a key step from chasing to leading.

一、工程建造技术

中国修建高铁面临的地质及气候非常复杂，在世界上没有成熟经验可借鉴，完全依靠自主创新形成了独特的技术优势。近年来中国建设了一大批适应高寒、高温、干旱、风沙等特殊气候环境，以及软土、黄土、季节性冻土、岩溶等复杂地质条件的高速铁路，是世界上唯一能在各种气候环境和复杂地质条件下建设高铁的国家。

中国拥有世界上最全面的桥梁设计建造技术、现代化的施工装备，修建了南京大胜关长江大桥、武汉天兴洲长江大桥等一批

1 Engineering & Construction

Due to the extremely complicated geological and climatic conditions in China for HSR construction, there is no ready experience to learn from other countries. China has gained unique technological advantages in HSR development through independent innovation. In recent years, China has built a number of HSRs adaptive to special climate conditions including alpine, high temperature, drought and sandstorm, as well as challenging geological conditions including soft soil, loess, seasonally frozen soil and Karst areas, becoming the only country in the world having

⊙无砟轨道
Ballastless Track

0372
0370

⊙南京大胜关长江大桥
Nanjing Dashengguan Yangtze River Bridge

跨越大江大河的世界级大跨度高速铁路桥梁。

中国掌握了在各种环境气候和复杂地质修建隧道技术，

the ability and experience in building HSRs in various climate and geological conditions.

China has the most comprehensive

bridge design & construction technologies and modernized construction equipment. A number of world-leading high-speed railway bridges with super long span have been built, such as Nanjing Dashengguan Yangtze River Bridge and Wuhan Tianxingzhou Yangtze River Bridge.

建成广深港高铁狮子洋隧道、西成高铁秦岭隧道群等万米以上隧道100余座。

中国掌握了铁路大型客站设计建造技术，突破了规划设计、空间结构、功能布局、流线组织等多个难题，实现了铁路与民航、地铁、市内道路的综合布局及各种交通运输方式之间的无缝换乘，实现了建筑风格与地域文化的有机融合，相继建成北京南站、武汉站、广州南站、上海虹桥站等一大批现代化综合客运枢纽，成为铁路形象的新窗口、城市发展的新门户。

⊙武汉站综合客运枢纽
Public Transportation Terminal (Wuhan Railway Station)

The construction technology of tunnels in various environments, climate and complex geology has been mastered in China. More than 100 tunnels over 10,000 meters have been built, such as Shiziyang Tunnel of Guangzhou-Shenzhen-Hong Kong High-Speed Railway and Qinling Tunnel Group of Xicheng High-Speed Railway.

China has mastered the design and construction technology of large railway passenger stations, and has broken through many difficult problems such as planning and design, spatial structure, functional layout, streamline organization, etc. It has realized the comprehensive layout of railway and civil aviation, subway, urban roads and seamless transfer between various modes of transportation, and has realized the organic combination of architectural style and regional culture. A large number of modern integrated passenger transport hubs, such as Beijingnan Railway Station, Wuhannan Railway Station, Guangzhounan Railway Station and Shanghai Hongqiao Railway Station, have been built one after another, which has become a new window for railway image and a new gateway for urban development.

◎杭黄高速铁路汤青山隧道
Hangzhou-Mount Huang High-Speed Railway (Tangqingshan Tunnel)

二、高速动车组技术

中国自2000年开始组织高速动车组研制开发，先后自主设计研制了先锋号、中华之星等动车组并上线进行了大量试验。2006年以来，在对世界先进动车组制造技术引进消化吸收再创新的基础上，批量生产投入运营了和谐型系列高速动车组。

2012年开始，中国全面启动中国标准动车组研制工作。2015年至2016年，中国标准动车组先后完成了型式试验、科学研究试验、运用考核，验证了中国标准动车组和关键系统功能性能。2017年6月，中国标准动车组被命名为复兴号并批量投入运营。

2 High-Speed Electrical Multiple Unit

The development of high-speed EMU in China started in 2000, since when the "Pioneer", the "Star of China" and other types of EMU trains were successively developed and put on lines for a large number of tests. A portfolio of EMU trains have been manufactured in batches and put into service since 2006 based on the introduction, digestion , absorption and re-innovation of advanced manufacturing technology of EMU trains around the world.

China initiated the development of China Standardized EMU in 2012, and completed required type test, scientific

复兴号动车组的安全性、经济性、舒适性、节能环保等性能大幅提升，表现出世界一流的卓越品质。列车设计寿命提高到30年，能够适应中国地域广阔、环境复杂、长距离、高强度运行的需求；采用全新低阻力流线型头型和车体平顺化设计，列车阻力

research test and application assessment test to validate its performance and key systems during 2015–2016. China Standardized EMU was named as Fuxing in June 2017 and put into commercial service in batches.

The Fuxing EMU shows outstanding performance in its substantially improved safety, cost-effectiveness,

⊙复兴号命名仪式
Fuxing EMU Naming Ceremony

降低7.5%～12.3%，能耗下降；列车容量更大，旅客乘坐空间更加宽敞；列车设置智能化感知系统，建立强大的安全监测系统，全车部署2500余项监测点，能够全方位实时监测。

基于复兴号平台，中国铁路持续开展技术创新，根据市场需

comfort, energy conservation and environment-friendliness. The train is designed with a prolonged life span of 30 years and can meet the operation needs of vast territory, complex environment, long distance and high frequency; the new type of streamlined train head and smooth car body reduce the train resistance by 7.5%–12.3%, leading to

⊙时速350公里复兴号动车组整装待发
350 km/h Fuxing EMUs Waiting for Departure

求研制不同速度等级、适应不同环境需求的系列化产品，不断完善复兴号动车组家族体系。

17辆编组时速350公里超长版复兴号动车组，载客能力较16辆编组提升了7.5%。该车已于2019年1月5日在北京至上海高速铁路上线运营，进一步提升京沪

a dramatic decline of energy consumption; a bigger inner space of train makes passengers more comfortable; with over 2,500 monitoring sensors deployed all over the train, the intelligent sensing system and powerful safety monitoring system can make full-coverage and real-time monitoring.

Based on Fuxing platform, China

⊙时速160公里动力集中复兴号动车组
160 km/h Power Centralized Fuxing EMUs

高铁等繁忙干线的运输能力。

时速160公里动力集中动车组按照动车组技术标准一体化设计和制造，适用于所有普速电气化铁路。该型动车组2019年1月上线以来，运营状态和性能表现良好，安全舒适性较好，被旅客昵称为“绿巨人”。

截至2018年底，中国铁路装备动车组3254组，其中复兴号动车组365组。

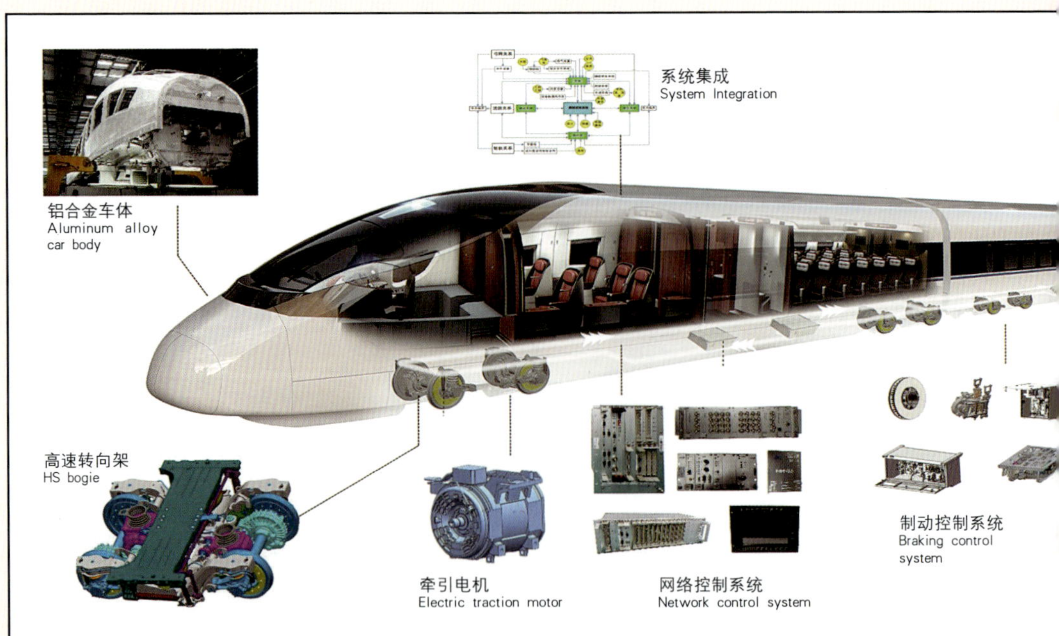

⊙复兴号动车组是由我国自主研发、具有完全知识产权的新一代高速列车
Fuxing EMUs are the new generation high-speed trains developed by China with complete domestic intellectual property rights.

Railway continues technological innovation, develops serialized products with different speed and different environmental needs, according to market demand.

Extra-long Fuxing EMU formed of 17-unit group leveled up by 7.5% compared with the 16-unit group. HSR started operation between Beijing and Shanghai on January 5, 2019, which will further enhance the transport capacity of busy lines such as Beijing-Shanghai, which will further enhance the transport capacity of busy lines such as Beijing-Shanghai HSR.

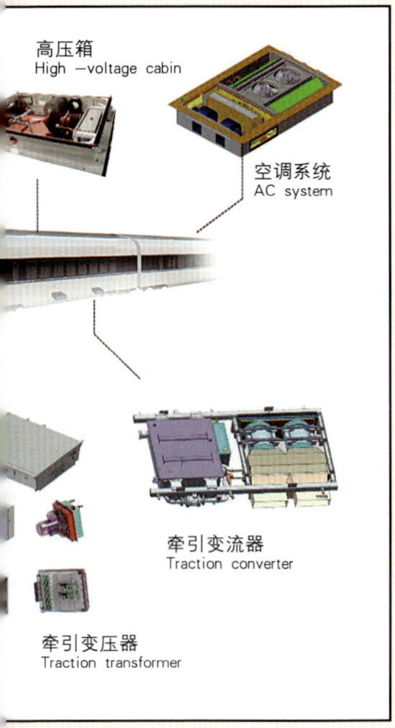

The 160 km/h power concentrated EMU is designed and manufactured in accordance with the EMU technical standards and is suitable for all general-speed electrified railways. Since its launch in January 2019, the EMU has been known as the "Hulk" by passengers because of its good performance, safety and comfort.

By the end of 2018, China railway is equipped with 3,254 high-speed EMU trains, including 365 Fuxing EMU trains.

⊙动车所内动车组存放夜景

The Night Scene of EMUs in Dynamic Vehicle Place

行车调度指挥中心
Train Dispatching Operation Command Center

计算机联锁系统
Computer Interlocking System

三、列车控制技术

列车运行控制系统被称为高速铁路的“大脑和中枢神经”，是保障行车安全和正点运行的关键系统，结构复杂、技术难度大。

列控中心
Train Control Center

2004年，中国构建了列车运行控制系统（CTCS）技术体系和总体框架，研发了应用于200～250km/h线路的CTCS−2、应用于300km/h及以上线路的CTCS−3级列控系统，能够满足不同速度等级高速动车组列车共线跨线运行控制需要。

轨道电路系统
Track Circuit System

经过多年的研究和运用，中国已掌握了高速

3 Train Control

The train operation control system, known as the “brain and central nervous system” of the HSR, is a major system guaranteeing safety and punctual operation of high speed trains. It has a complex structure and is full of technical difficulties.

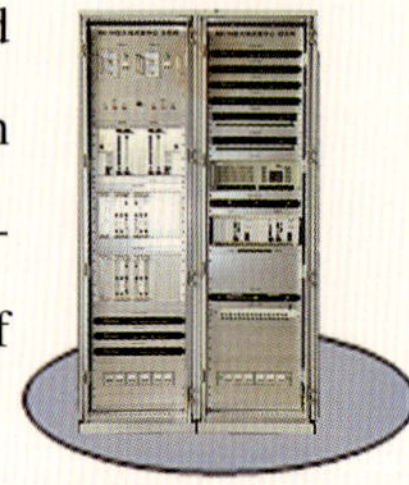
无线闭塞中心
Radio Block Center

In 2004, China built the technical system and general framework for train operation control system (CTCS), and developed CTCS-2 and CTCS-3 systems respectively for railway lines with a design speed of 200–250 km/h and those with a design speed of 300 km/h and above, which enable trains to share the same line or EMU trains at higher speed to run on lines with lower design speed.

应答器地面控制设备
Ground Control Equipment of Balise

After years of

信号机
Signal

列控系统地面设备
Field Devices of Train Control System

信号机
Signal

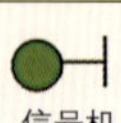
应答器
Balise

信号机
Signal

铁路列车控制系统核心技术，开发了具有自主知识产权的列控系统全套装备，达到世界先进水平。

research and practice, China has mastered the core technology of HSR train control system and developed a whole set of train control equipment with intellectual property rights, which has reached world's advanced level.

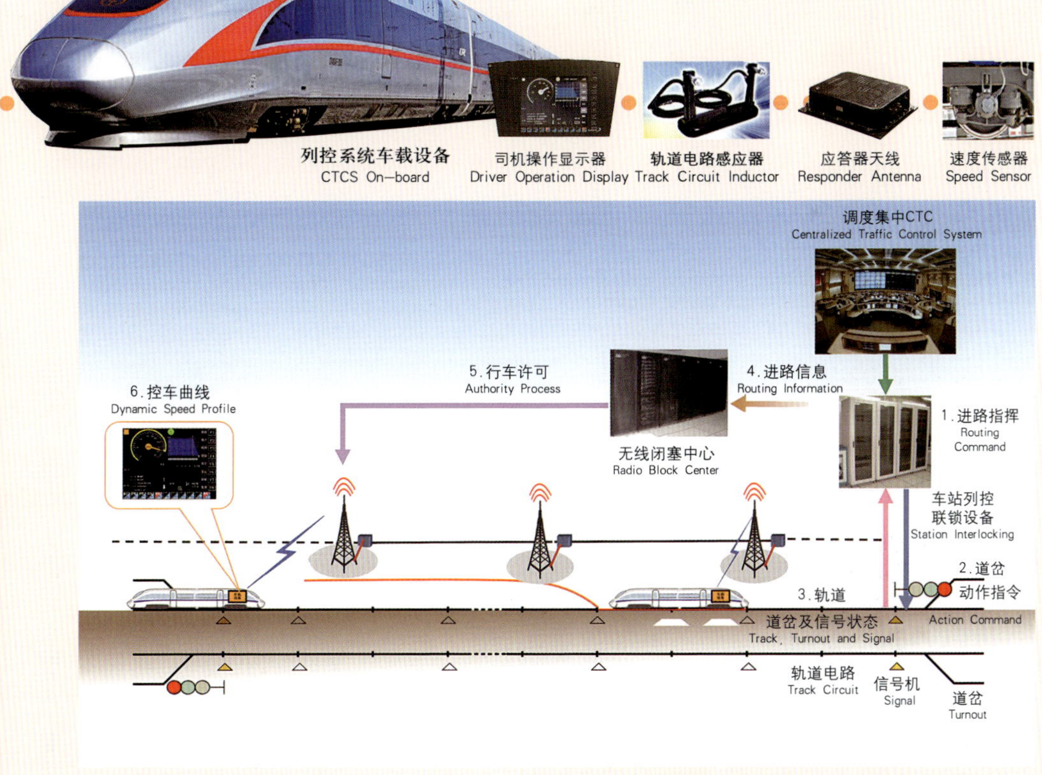

⊙中国列车运行控制系统
Chinese Train Control System (CTCS)

四、牵引供电技术

中国成功研制并应用大张力接触网、高强度接触导线和远程监控等成套装备，形成了能够满足动车组长大编组和重联运行、3分钟追踪，持续时速350公里双弓稳定受流和安全可靠运行的供电系统，建成了世界上规模最大的高速铁路牵引供电数据采集与监视控制系统（SCADA），牵引供电整体技术达到世界领先水平。

4 Traction Power Supply

China has successfully developed and applied a complete set of equipment including high-tension OCS, high-strength contact wire and remote monitoring, established a safe and reliable power supply system which fulfills coupled and long-formation EMUs operation under 3-minute headway as well as continuous and stable current-feeding by double pantographs at the speed of 350 km/h, and built the world's largest SCADA system. The traction power supply technology has reached world's leading level.

⊙高铁供电接触网技术
Overhead Contact Lines

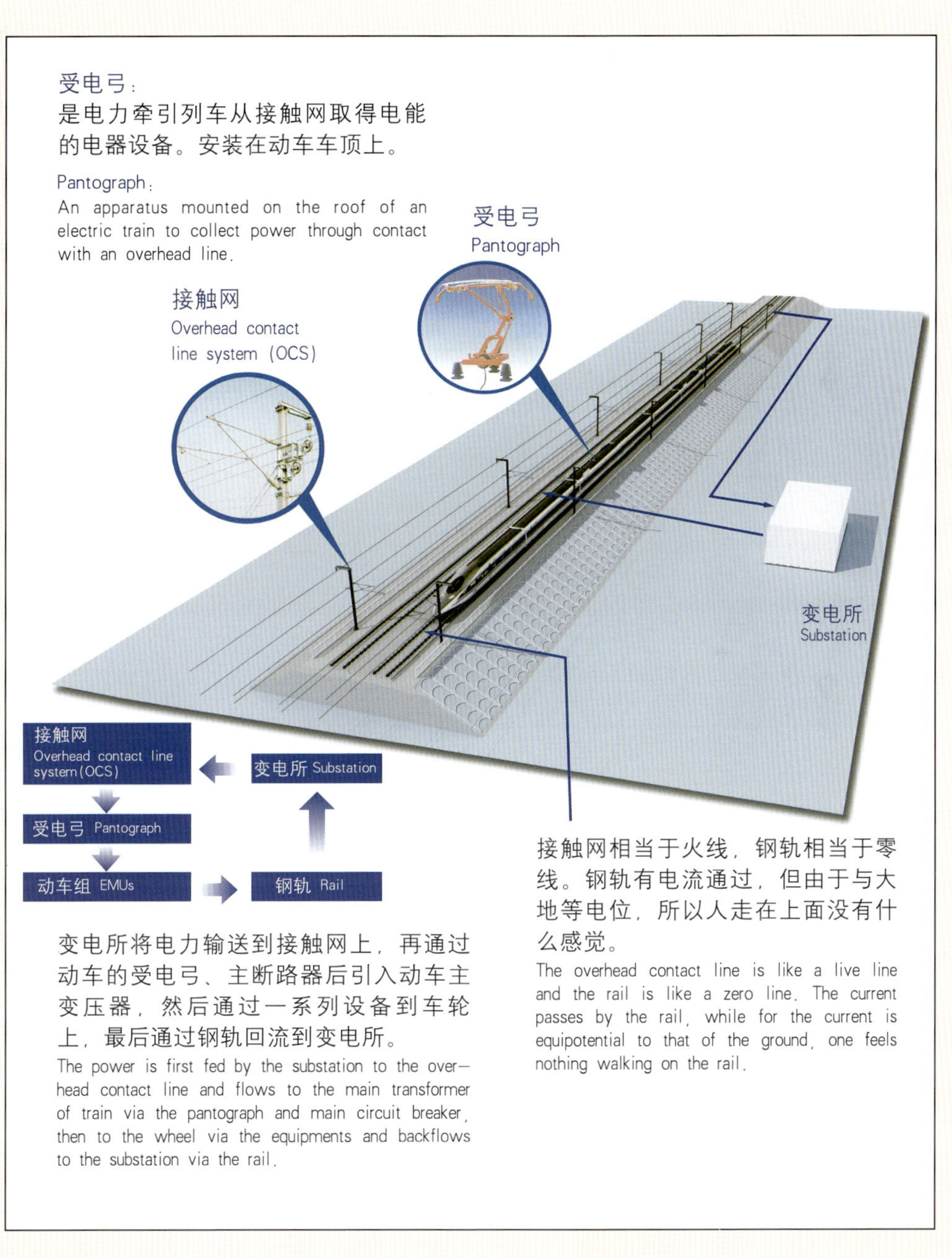

受电弓：
是电力牵引列车从接触网取得电能的电器设备。安装在动车车顶上。

Pantograph：
An apparatus mounted on the roof of an electric train to collect power through contact with an overhead line.

变电所将电力输送到接触网上，再通过动车的受电弓、主断路器后引入动车主变压器，然后通过一系列设备到车轮上，最后通过钢轨回流到变电所。

The power is first fed by the substation to the overhead contact line and flows to the main transformer of train via the pantograph and main circuit breaker, then to the wheel via the equipments and backflows to the substation via the rail.

接触网相当于火线，钢轨相当于零线。钢轨有电流通过，但由于与大地等电位，所以人走在上面没有什么感觉。

The overhead contact line is like a live line and the rail is like a zero line. The current passes by the rail, while for the current is equipotential to that of the ground, one feels nothing walking on the rail.

⊙调度指挥中心
Dispatch and Command Center

五、运营管理技术

中国拥有世界上规模最大的高速铁路网，构建了中国国家铁路集团有限公司、各铁路局集团有限公司和车站的三级高速铁路调度指挥体系，掌握了复杂路网条件下高铁列车运行计划编制和

5 Operation Management

China has the world's largest HSR network. A three-level HSR traffic control system consisting of CHINA RAILWAY, regional railway group corporations and stations has been established. China has mastered the integrated dispatching technologies for EMU application, which can accommo-

动车组运用综合调度技术，解决了不同动车组编组、不同速度、不同距离、跨线运行等运输组织难题，实现了列车运行设计最小追踪间隔3～5分钟。每天安全有序地组织着5600至6500多列动车组列车开行。

date the requirements of HSR operation plan, and thus solved the difficulties in dispatching HSR trains with different formations, speeds, running distances, or trains with different speeds sharing the same line. The design minimum headway can achieve 3–5 minutes, with daily operation number of EMU trains from 5,600 to more than 6,500.

六、风险防控技术

中国构建了闭环管理的高速铁路安全保障体系，通过固定设施及移动装备实时监测检测、防灾安全监控、机械化养护维修等措施，可对高铁运行进行全过程跟踪监测、全系统定期检测。

6 Risk Prevention and Control

The China HSR safety system with closed-loop management is established to conduct whole-process tracing and monitoring of train operation and regular checking of all systems to ensure the operation safety of HSRs via monitoring and inspection on track and train, disaster prevention monitoring, mechanized maintenance and other approaches.

⊙高铁综合检测车

High-Speed Comprehensive Inspection Train

1706

第4章 中国高速铁路主要特点

Chapter 4 Main Features

经过多年的建设和运营管理实践,中国高速铁路安全可靠、平稳舒适、方便快捷、节能环保、适用性强等特点日益凸显。

Years of construction, operation and management practices have increasingly highlighted the major technological and economic characteristics of China's HSR system. China's HSR system is safe and reliable, smooth and comfortable , environment-friendly and exceptional applicability.

一、安全可靠

中国建设了稳固耐久的路基、桥梁、隧道等高速铁路线路基础设施，制造了安全可靠的高速列车，建立了性能可靠的牵引供电、通信信号等高速铁路控制系统。经过多年的运营实践，形成了基础设施、移动装备、综合检测、防灾减灾、应急救援为一体的安全风险管理体系，确保了高速列车的安全运行。

中国高速铁路实行全线封闭管理，具有先进的自然灾害及异物侵限监测系统和完善的灾害预防措

1 Safe and Reliable

China has built a solid and durable line infrastructure including sub-grades, bridges, tunnels, manufactured safe and reliable high-speed trains, and developed reliable control system including traction, power supply, communications & signaling etc. After years of operation practice, a safety and risk management system integrating infrastructure, moving equipment, comprehensive inspection, disaster prevention and relieving and emergency rescue has been established to guarantee the safe operation of high-speed trains.

The HSRs are fully-fenced and equipped with advanced safety monitor-

⊙复兴号列车运行试验
Operation Test

⊙供电接触网检修
OCS Repair

施、应急救援措施，能够及时发现和处理大风、降雨、冰雪、地震等自然灾害和突发事件。

中国高速铁路构建了人防、物防、技防“三位一体”安全保障体系，充分运用物联网、大数据、北斗卫星定位等现代科技手段，提升高铁设备监测检测、风险预警和养护维修的智能化、科学化水平。动车组司机不仅经过

⊙机械师检查动车组轮对
Inspectors Check the EMU Wheels

ing system and complete prevention and rescue measures against disasters, which can timely identify and deal with natural disasters and emergencies such as heavy wind, rain, ice, snow and earthquakes.

China's HSR safety system is an integrated risk control and prevention system that includes safety approaches in three aspects: human, equipment and technology. Within this system, modern technologies such as networking, big data, Beidou satellite positioning are used to make equipment

⊙动车组司机在模拟仿真系统上进行实操培训
EMU Drivers Practice with the Simulation Training System

严格选拔，而且每年组织培训，全面提升司机标准化作业和安全保障能力。

monitoring & inspection, risk pre-alarming and maintenance more scientific and intelligent. EMU drivers are selected through strict evaluation procedures and must receive training per year, in a bid to enhance their abilities of regulated and standardized operation , promote safety and security capability.

⊙动车组列车员在多媒体教室培训
EMU Stewardesses Receive Training in Multi-Media Classroom

二、平稳舒适

中国自主创新的钢轨、无缝线路、无砟轨道和高速道岔等技术，保证了高速铁路线路的高平顺性，使动车组运行更加平稳安全。

中国高速动车组采用了减振性能良好的高速转向架，车厢内

2 Smooth and Comfortable

Technologies independently developed by China for rail, seamless track, ballast-less track, high-speed turnouts, etc., ensure the smoothness of HSRs. That's more stable and safer for EMU operation.

China's high-speed EMU trains are equipped with high-speed bogies with excellent vibration—damping performance

⊙服务旅客
Service to Passengers

振动小。车内采用的是舒适的软座椅，车窗大、采光好、视野开阔。全自动恒温空调系统能够为旅客提供适宜的车内环境温度、湿度和清新空气。动车组车厢内设有轮椅存放区、婴儿护理桌、残障人卫生间等，可以满足不同旅客的需要。动车组的地板与站台可以良好对接，代步工具能够无障碍上下车，为旅客提供了平稳舒适的旅行环境。

to reduce inside vibration and noise. Cushioned seats provide comfort while wide windows provide adequate natural lighting and broad view. The fully-automatic constant temperature air conditioning system brings moderate temperature, humidity, together with fresh air. Wheelchair storage area, baby-sitting tables and accessible restrooms can also be found inside the train to meet the different needs of passengers. Train floor is well connected to the platform so that all kinds of conveyance can easily move onto and off the train without any trouble. All these ensure smooth and comfortable travel environment for the passengers.

⊙热情周到的服务
Warm and Considerate Service

三、方便快捷

中国高速铁路车站安装了人脸识别、智能导航等先进的旅客自助服务系统，方便旅客进出站、候车和换乘。采用人性化无障碍设计，在通往候车室、站台

3 Fast and Convenient

HSR stations are equipped with advanced self-service systems such as face recognition and smart navigation to facilitate entrance into/exit from stations, waiting and transfers. Human-oriented accessible designs for the disabled can

⊙人脸识别进站
Face Identification System

等服务设施的地面设置了盲道，设有残障人士专用服务设施，普遍设置爱心服务区，为重点旅客提供温馨服务。按照零距离换乘理念，通过精心合理的场、站布局，建设现代化客运枢纽和旅

be found in stations, including tactile paving to help the visually handicapped navigate to waiting halls and platforms, and special service facilities for the disabled. Caring service zones are located in most stations to provide thoughtful services for passengers in need. Based

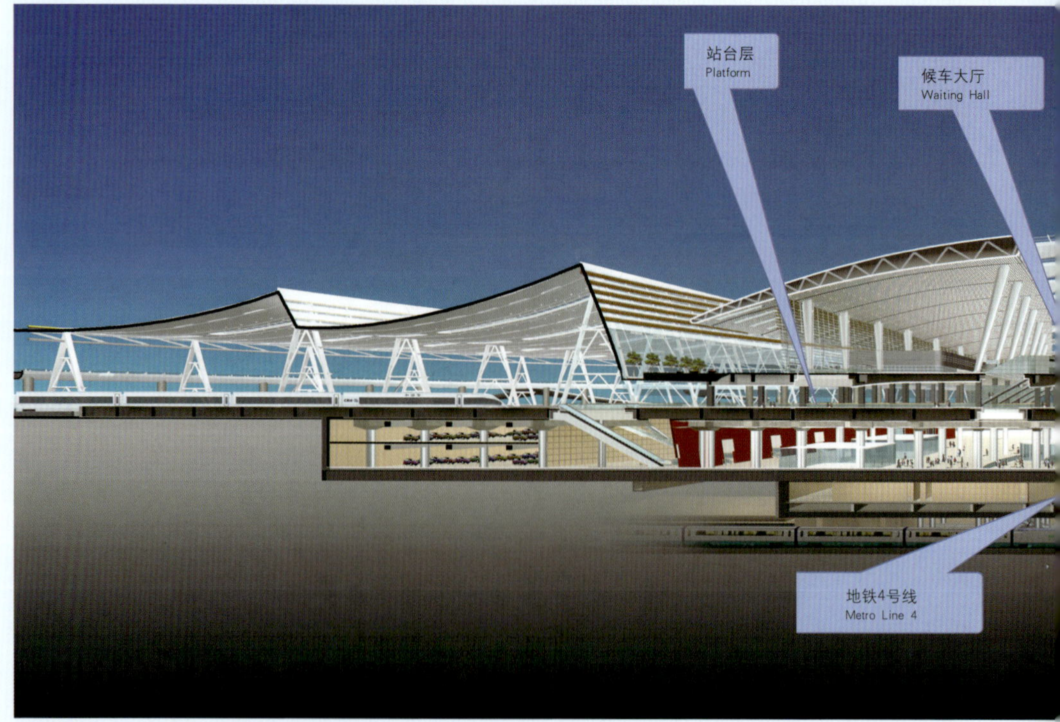

⊙北京南站“零距离换乘”示意图
Graph Showing "Zero-distance Transfer" in Beijingnan Railway Station

客中转换乘中心，使高速铁路客站与城市公交系统甚至机场融为一体，方便旅客在站内顺畅换乘地铁、公共汽车等交通工具。

中国铁路积极推进“高铁网+互联网”双网融合，旅客既

on the concept of zero-distance transfer, HSR stations are closely integrated with urban public transport systems, or even airports through considerate and rational arrangement of stations and depots, to develop modern passenger transport hubs and transfer centres where pas-

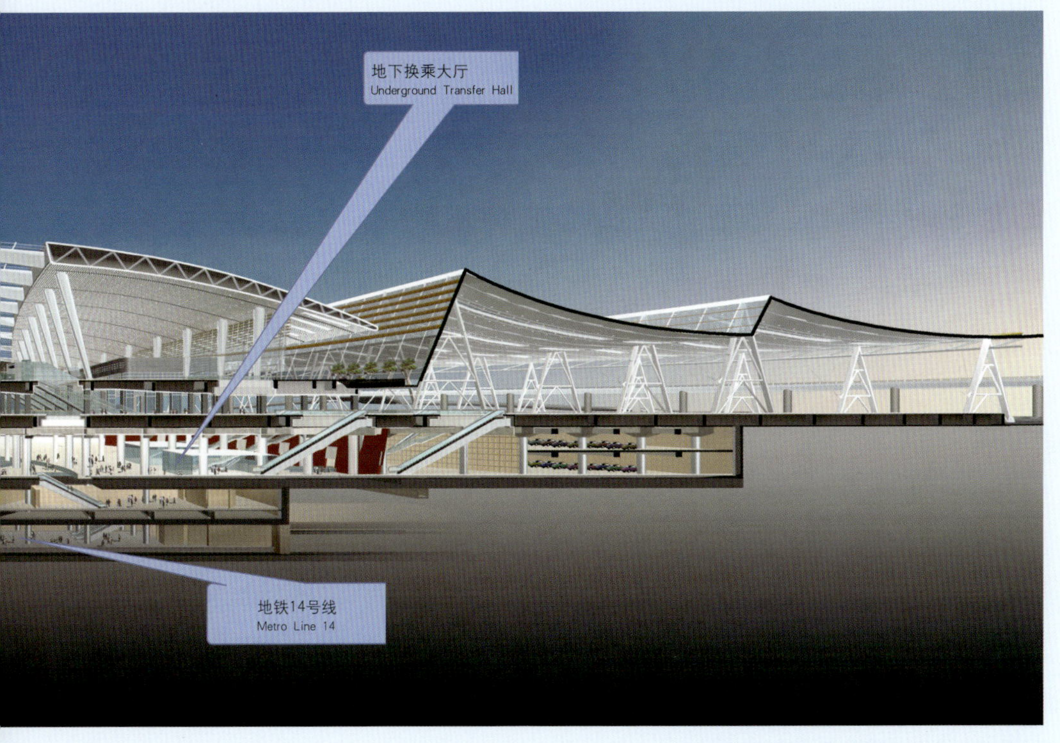

可以在互联网上登录中国铁路客户服务中心网站（http://www.12306.cn）、手机客户端或通过自助语音电话95105105购（订）票，也可以在铁路车站的人工售票窗口、自动售票机、火车票代售处购买高铁车票。购票时可选择现金、银行卡、微信、支付宝等不同方式支付票款。2018年12306互联网售票超过28亿张，日售票能力达到1500万张，高峰时每秒售票量达1000

⊙铁路12306手机购票客户端
12306 China Railway APP

sengers can quickly transfer to subways, public buses or other vehicles.

Integration of high-speed network with the Internet has been actively promoted. Passengers can get or order high-speed train tickets easily through the website of China Railway Customer Service Center (http://www.12306.cn), mobile App, voice call (95105105) at ticket windows in stations, self-service ticketing machines at stations, or ticket agencies. Multiple payment options are available including cash, bank card, Wechat and Alipay. Through the internet ticketing system, over 2.8 billion tickets are sold in 2018, with the maximum number of daily sold tickets reaching 15 million and 1,000 tickets per second during peak times.

⊙南昌站自动售票处
Automatic Ticket Machine in Nanchang Railway Station

⊙车站窗口购票
Passengers Buy Tickets at the Ticket Window

张，已成为世界上规模最大的实时票务交易系统。高铁站车正逐步实现Wi-Fi信号覆盖，已推出了网上订餐、接续换乘、自主选座、移动支付、行程提醒、常旅客、共享汽车、便民托运等服务。

自2018年以来，海南环岛、上海至南京、成都至重庆、广州至珠海（湛江西）、昆明至大理至丽江等多条高铁（城际铁路）开展电子客票

The 12306 system has become the largest real-time ticketing system in the world. Increasing number of high-speed trains and stations has been covered with Wi-Fi services. Services including online meal ordering, connecting tickets, seat selection, online payment, trip reminding, frequent passenger service, car sharing and luggage consignment are provided to

⊙刷二代身份证出站
Passengers Can Use 2G ID Card to Enter/Exit the Station

⊙为旅客提供温馨服务
Warm Service for Passengers

⊙高铁互联网订餐交接
Meal Ordering Online and Meal Service

⊙高铁+共享汽车
High-Speed Railway & Car Sharing

应用试点。

中国高速铁路服务品质已达到国际先进水平。

passengers.

Since 2018, many high-speed railways (inter-city railways) such as Hainan Island High-Speed Loop Line, Beijing-Nanjing line, Chengdu-Chongqing

⊙沪宁城际试点电子客票应用

Trial Application of E-Ticket in Shanghai-Nanjing Intercity HSR

line, Guangzhou-Zhuhai (Zhanjiangxi) line, Kunming-Dali-Lijiang line, etc. have been experimenting with the application of E-Tickets.

The service quality of China's high-speed railway has reached the international advanced level.

⊙为外国旅客提供温馨服务
Warm Service for Foreign Passengers

四、节能环保

合理选线保护生态环境。在线路设计时，充分利用既有交通廊道，减少对城市的分割和土地占用；对沿线自然保护区、风景名胜区、水源保护区等，高铁线路尽量绕避，保护生态环境。例如：西成高铁在穿越秦岭山脉过程中，采取隧道群方式穿越，隧道长度达110公里，埋深在800米至1000米，最大限度保护了大熊猫、羚牛、金丝猴等野生动物栖息环境。

以桥代路节约土地资源。在有条件、可实施地段采用了占地少的架桥修建高速铁路的方案，与6米填高的路基相比，每

4 Energy Efficient and Environment-Friendly

Alignments are chosen rationally to protect ecological environment. Existing transport corridors are fully used during route design in order to reduce city division and land occupation. In addition, great effort is taken to avoid natural reserves, places of interest and water sources, so as to protect ecological environment. For instance, Xi'an-Chengdu HSR crosses Qinling Mountains through tunnel clusters with a total length of 110 km and burial depths of 800 m to 1,000 m, to best protect the habitats of pandas, takins, golden monkeys and other wildlife.

Bridges are used instead of subgrades to save land resources. Less-land-occupying HSR bridges are built in sections with appropriate conditions and

⊙京广高速铁路北京西至涿州东间
Beijing-Guangzhou High-Speed Railway (Beijingxi-Zhuozhoudong)

⊙西安至成都高速铁路
Xi' an-Chengdu High-Speed Railway

公里桥梁可节约土地约55亩。例如：京沪高铁桥梁长度占线路总长的81.5%，哈大高铁桥梁长度占线路总长的72%，京津城际铁路桥梁长度占线路总长的87%，由于在线路设计中提高了桥梁比例，节约了大量土地资源。

高速铁路采用电力牵引，消

feasibility. Compared with 6-meter high sub-grade, each kilometer of bridge saves about 55 mu (3.67 hectares) of land. For example, bridges take up 81.5% of the total length of Beijing-Shanghai HSR, 72% of that of Harbin-Dalian HSR, and 87% of that of Beijing-Tianjin Inter-city Railway. Higher proportion of bridges in HSR design helps to save a large amount of land.

HSRs employ electric power traction

⊙上海虹桥站屋顶太阳能装备
Solar Panels on the Roof of Shanghai Hongqiao Station

除了油烟、粉尘和其他废气对环境的影响。高铁车站大量采用节能技术，其墙体、屋顶选用节能新型材料，照明充分利用自然光并采用高效节能灯及智能控制新技术。例如：利用上海虹桥站无柱雨棚屋面6.1万平方米，铺设了23910块太阳能电池板，实现年均发电630万度。

and therefore are free of impact on the environment by oil fumes, dusts and other waste gases. Multiple energy—saving technologies are adopted in the development of HSR stations. New type energy-saving materials are used for station walls and roofs, while natural lighting is made full use of together with energy-efficient lamps and intelligent technologies to provide illumination. Taking Shanghai Hongqiao Railway Station as an

⊙小鸟天堂：广州至湛江高速铁路全封闭声屏障
Bird's Paradise: Full-enclosed Noise Barrier on Guangzhou-Zhanjiang High-Speed Railway

高速动车组均采用密闭式集便装置，卫生间污物收集到集便装置污物箱中，到车站或动车段（所）后，利用地面吸污装置集中收集处理。这样既方便了旅客，又保护了铁路沿线环境。

example, 23,910 solar panels are installed on the roof of the 61,000-square-meter column-free rainshed , which produce 6.3 million kWh of power per year.

Sealed waste-collection devices are installed on EMU trains to store toilet sewage in the waste containers of the devices before such sewage are further collected for treatment by trackside sewage suction devices in stations or EMU depots. This method is convenient for passengers and preserves the environment along the railway.

⊙动车组列车吸污作业
Vacuum Waste Collection for EMU

五、适用性强

中国高速动车组能够适应各种复杂气候和环境，有时速160公里、200～250公里和300～350公里三种速度等级，设有一等、二等、商务等车厢和适宜长途旅行的卧铺动车组；适应不同运输需求的8辆、16辆和17辆三种固定编组，其中两列8辆编组动车组可重联运行。

5 Exceptional Applicability

China's high-speed EMUs are adaptable to various complex climates and environments. Trains are operated at three different grades of speed, 160km/h, 200–250km/h and 300–350 km/h, with seats divided into business-class, first-class and second-class, or even with sleeping cars suitable for long-distance journey. To meet different transport needs, there are three kinds of high-

⊙商务座
Business-class

中国高速铁路采用高密度、公交化的开行方式，始发、运行、到达正点率分别平均达到99%、98%、97%以上。

⊙一等座
First-class

⊙二等座
Second-class

speed EMU trains with different fixed composition: 8-car trains, 16-car trains, and 17-car trains. Moreover, two 8-car trains can be coupled together to operate.

China's high-speed railways adopt high-density and public transport mode of operation, with the average starting, running and arriving punctuality rates of 99%, 98% and 97% respectively.

⊙餐吧车
Food Bar Cars

⊙卧铺动车组
Sleeping Cars

⊙卧铺动车组洗手台
Washstand on Sleeper EMU

第5章 中国高速铁路为人民创造美好生活

Chapter 5 Better Lives for People

目前，中国“四纵四横”高铁网已经提前建成运营，“八纵八横”高铁网正在不断延展。长三角、珠三角、京津冀三大城市群高铁已连片成网，东部、中部、西部和东北四大板块实现高铁互联互通，不仅极大方便了旅客出行，而且打开了广大人民群众美好旅行生活的新空间，受到越来越多人们的青睐，正在改变中国人的出行方式，助推中国经济社会持续健康发展。

At present, Chinese four horizontal and four vertical national railway network started operation ahead of schedule. Moreover, the construction of eight horizontal and eight vertical national railway network has fully launched. HSRs weaved a network covering China's three city clusters, namely the Yangtze River Delta, the Pearl River Delta and Beijing-Tianjin-Hebei. Four regions in China—East, Middle, West, and Northeast China are now connected by such network, which not only has greatly facilitated passengers' travel, but also opens up a new space for the people to enjoy a better traveling life. The safe, punctual, fast, comfortable and environmental-friendly HSRs favored by more and more people are changing the Chinese people's traveling habits while promoting sustainable and sound development of Chinese economy and the society.

一、高速铁路极大方便了人们出行

有了高铁，春运压力极大缓解，乡愁不再遥远，回家之路更加顺畅；有了高铁，人们的出行更加便捷高效，乘火车同等距离出行的时间普遍比过去压缩一半以上；有了高铁，蜀道不再难，西安至成都高铁、重庆至贵阳铁

1 Convenient Travel

With high-speed railway, the pressure of Spring Festival travel is greatly relieved, the way home is no longer far away and more smooth. With high-speed railway, the pace of travel is more efficient, and the travel time by train at the same distance is generally less than half in the past. With high-speed railway, the Sichuan road is no longer difficult. The railways make it easier for passengers

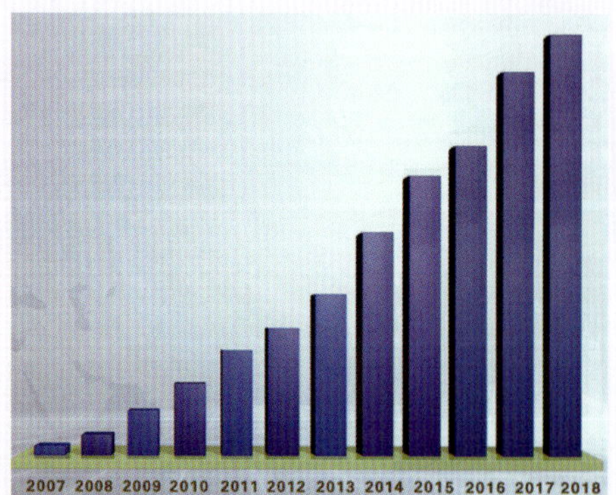

⊙动车组列车累计发送旅客96亿人
The CRH Trains Have Transported 9.6 Billion Passengers in Total

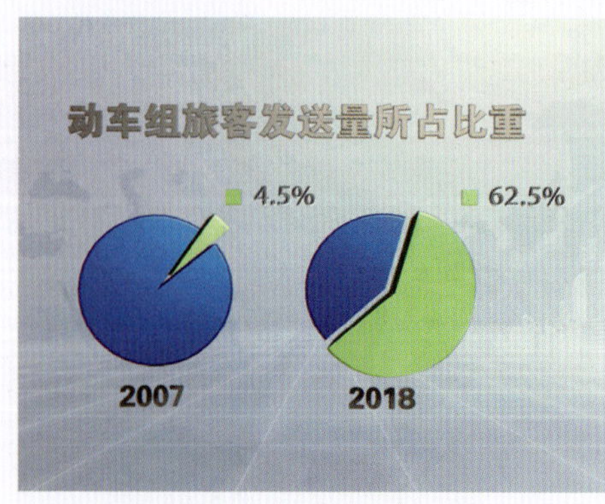

⊙动车组旅客发送量所占比重增大
Increased Proportion of Passenger Volume Carried by EMU

路、成都至重庆高铁让旅客可以方便快捷进出川渝地区。目前，中国每天开行动车组列车达到5600至6500多列，京津、沪宁、广深等多个地区实现高铁“公交化”出行。截至2018年底，动车组列车累计发送旅客96亿人次。

to get in and out of Sichuan and Chongqing, such as the Xi'an-Chengdu high-speed railway, the Chongqing-Guiyang railway and the Chengdu-Chongqing high-speed railway. Currently, 5,600-6,500 high-speed trains are operated daily. High-speed trains are dispatched like buses, such as Beijing-Tianjin,

⊙ 旅客在天津站乘车
Travel at Tianjin Railway Station

二、高速铁路带来了“同城效应”

高速铁路极大拉近了时空距离，促进了高铁沿线城市的交流，带来了“同城效应”，促进了城市群发展，也改变了不少年轻人的工作方式和老年人的养老方式，催生了高铁通勤族。高速铁路加快了东、中、西部和东北地区的交流，促进了区域经济社会协调发展，带来了“同域效应”，有力促进京津冀、粤港澳大湾区等地区一体化发展和长江经济带、西部大开发等区域发展战略的实施。相关机构研究表明，通高铁的城市与不通高铁的城市相比，可持续竞争力高出57%。

Shanghai-Nanjing, Guangzhou-Shenzhen lines. By the end of 2018, the total number of passengers carried by EMU trains reached 9.6 billion.

2 The same City Integration Effect

The HSR trains have greatly cut the travel time between cities, which promoted the exchanges between cities along the HSR lines, brought about the "city integration effect", and promoted the development of urban agglomeration. Many young people's working style and the elderly retired life have also been changed, which led to the birth of high-speed railway commuters. The HSR trains have accelerated the exchanges among the eastern, central, western and north-eastern regions, promoted the coordinated development of regional economy and society, brought about the "domain effect" and effectively promoted the implementation of regional development strategies, such as the integration of Beijing, Tianjin, Hebei and the integration of Guangdong, Hong Kong and Macao, and the Yangtze River Economic Belt and the Western Development. Research by relevant institutions shows that cities with high-speed rail lines are 57% more sustainable than those without HSR lines.

⊙大西高铁拉近了沿线城市时空
Datong-Xi'an HSR draws closer the time and space of the cities along the line.

三、"高铁+旅游"催生旅游新业态

乘着高铁去旅游，使"快旅慢游"成为可能，同等时间可以看到更多祖国大好河山，提升了旅游效率。高铁，让更多远在"深闺"、过去由于交通不便不易到达的旅游资源得以开发，许多地方出现"井喷式"增长。陕西佛坪、湖北恩施、安徽绩溪、广西三江、云南普者黑等地旅游接待人数的快速增长，均得益于高铁的开

3 Cultivating New Form of Tourism

Travelling by HSR trains makes it possible to "fast arrival and taking a slow tour". With the same period of time, we can see more beautiful rivers and mountains of our motherland, which improves the efficiency of tourism. HSR lines have enabled more tourism resources that were not easily accessible in the past due to inconvenient transportation to be exploited. Blowout-like growth has occurred in many places. The fast growth of tourist reception in Foping , Enshi, Jixi, Sanjiang , Puzhehei and other sce-

通。“高铁+旅游”，已经成为旅游发展新业态和人们旅游的新方式。

nic spots all benefited from the opening of HSR. “HSR+ tourism” has become a new form of tourism development and a new way of people’s tourism.

⊙乘高铁去旅游
Travel by High-Speed Train

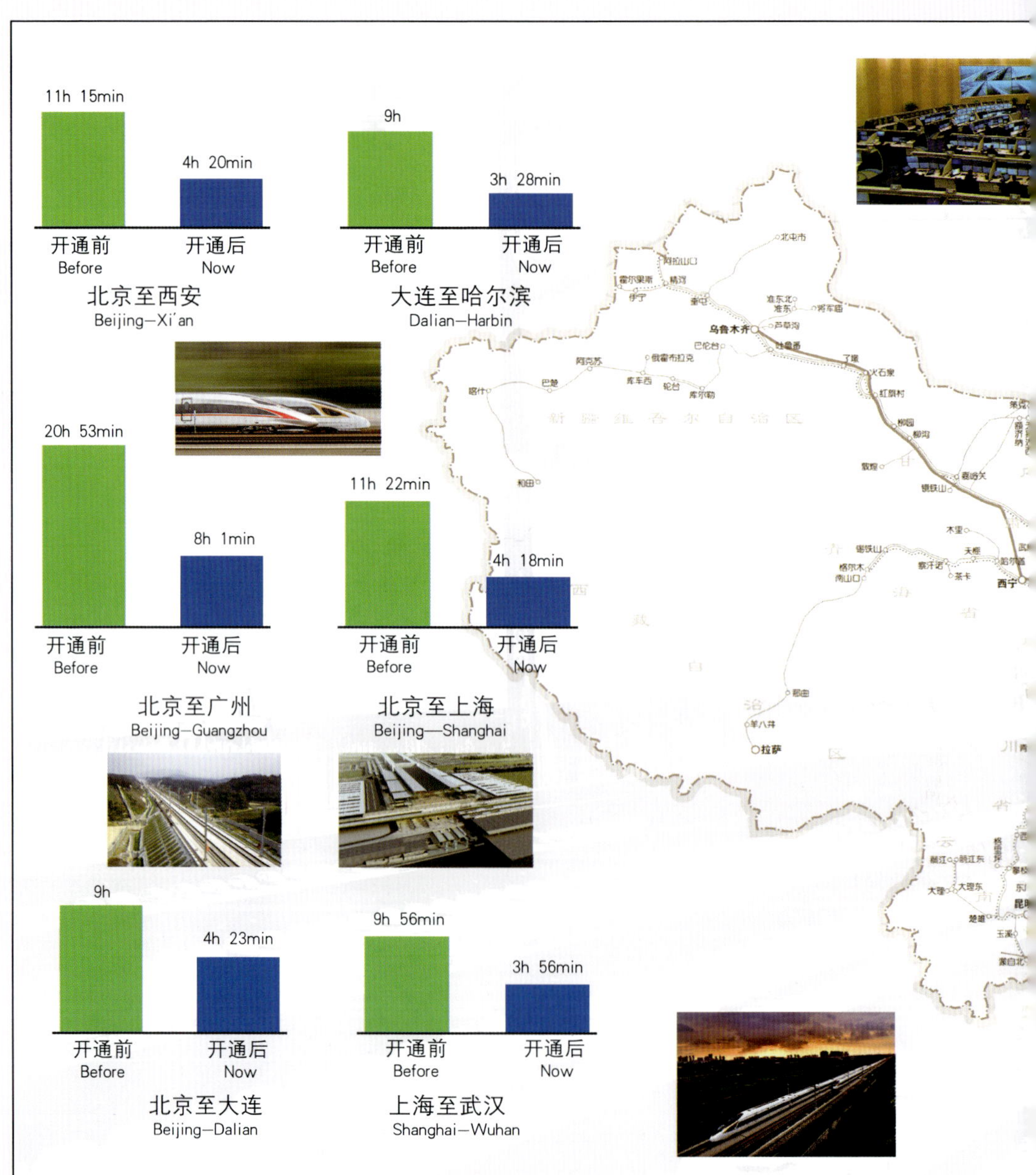

⊙高速铁路拉近城市间距离

High-Speed Railways Shorten Distances between Cities

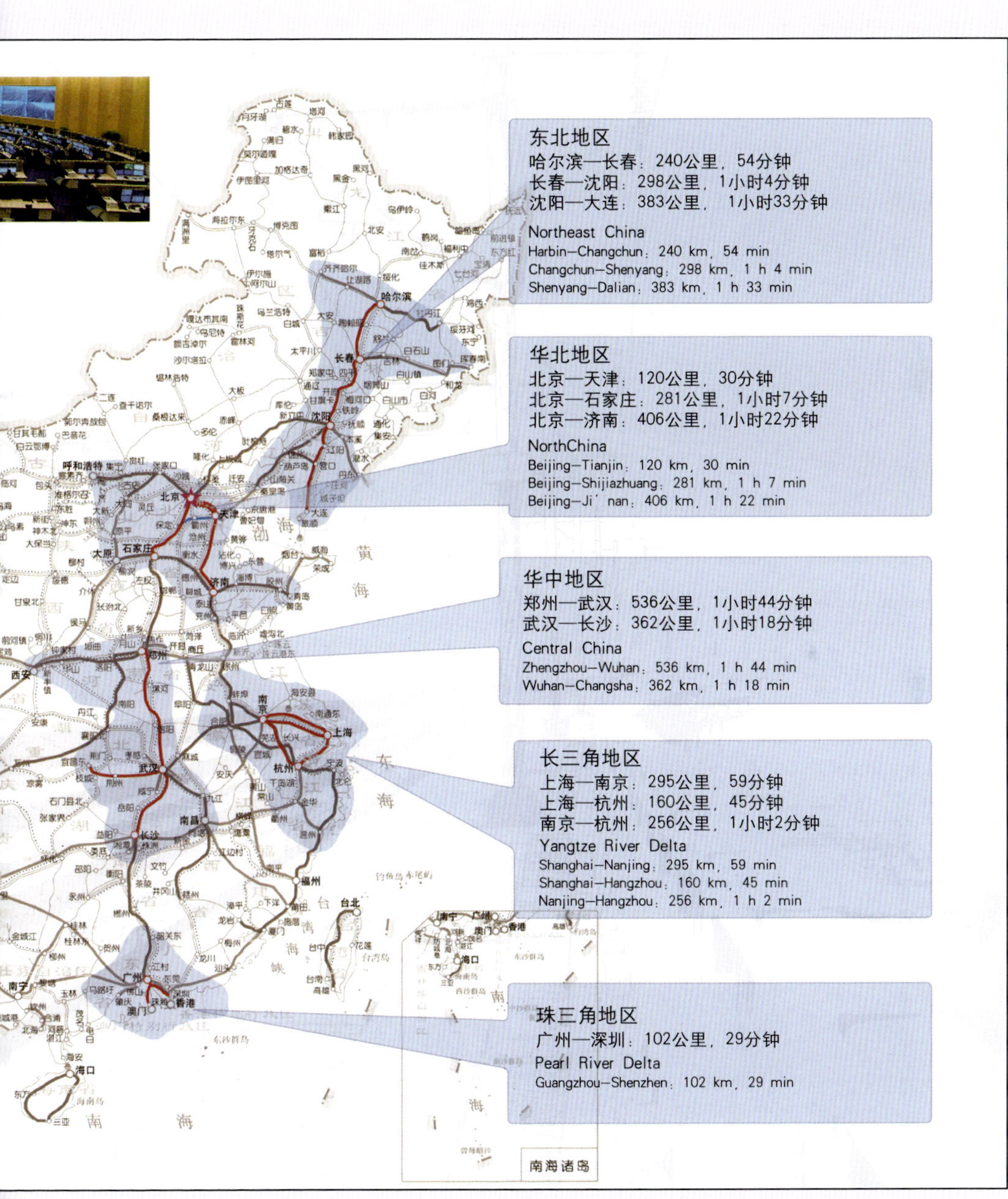
东北地区
哈尔滨—长春：240公里，54分钟
长春—沈阳：298公里，1小时4分钟
沈阳—大连：383公里，1小时33分钟
Northeast China
Harbin–Changchun：240 km，54 min
Changchun–Shenyang：298 km，1 h 4 min
Shenyang–Dalian：383 km，1 h 33 min
华北地区
北京—天津：120公里，30分钟
北京—石家庄：281公里，1小时7分钟
北京—济南：406公里，1小时22分钟
NorthChina
Beijing–Tianjin：120 km，30 min
Beijing–Shijiazhuang：281 km，1 h 7 min
Beijing–Ji' nan：406 km，1 h 22 min
华中地区
郑州—武汉：536公里，1小时44分钟
武汉—长沙：362公里，1小时18分钟
Central China
Zhengzhou–Wuhan：536 km，1 h 44 min
Wuhan–Changsha：362 km，1 h 18 min
长三角地区
上海—南京：295公里，59分钟
上海—杭州：160公里，45分钟
南京—杭州：256公里，1小时2分钟
Yangtze River Delta
Shanghai–Nanjing：295 km，59 min
Shanghai–Hangzhou：160 km，45 min
Nanjing–Hangzhou：256 km，1 h 2 min
珠三角地区
广州—深圳：102公里，29分钟
Pearl River Delta
Guangzhou–Shenzhen：102 km，29 min
哈尔滨
长春
沈阳
大连
北京
天津
石家庄
济南
郑州
武汉
长沙
南京
上海
杭州
广州
香港
澳门
西安
南昌
福州
台北
海口
南宁
南海诸岛

⊙沪昆高速铁路穿过贵州省凯里市境内长滩苗寨
Shanghai-Kunming High-Speed Railway (Changtan Miao Village)

四、高速铁路助力精准脱贫

中国中西部地区高速铁路发展迅速，相继建成了兰新、贵广、云桂、西成等一批高速铁路。截至2018年底，中西部地区高铁营业里程19862公里，占全国高铁总里程的66.4%。高速铁

4 Contributing to Targeted Poverty Alleviation

High-speed railways in central and western China have developed rapidly, and a number of high-speed railways, such as Lanzhou-Urumqi, Guiyang-Guangzhou, Nanning-Kunming and Xi'an-Chengdu, ,have been built successively. By the end of 2018, the operating mileage in the central and western regions was 19,862 km, accounting for 66.4% of the total mileage of high-speed railways in China. High-speed railways have greatly promoted the economic and social development of remote and poor areas, facilitated the travel of the people along the lines, and also increased the sale of agricultural products and attracting investment. High-speed railways

路极大地促进了边远贫困地区经济社会发展，方便了沿线群众出行，促进了农产品销售和招商引资，高铁成为沿线人民的致富线、幸福线。

中国在贫困地区设立高速铁路无轨站，扩大了高铁辐射范围，旅客在无轨站可以购买高铁

bring wealth and happiness to the people along the line.

China has set up high-speed railway trackless stations in poor areas, expanding the radiation scope of HSR. Passengers can buy tickets at the stations, and connect to stations by bus easily. The modern high-speed railway has greatly improved the local transportation environment and

⊙广西壮族自治区凌云县高速铁路“无轨站”
Trackless Station of Lingyun Country High-Speed Railway

车票，通过公交接驳至高铁，将贫困地区人民与现代高铁相连，极大地改善了当地交通环境，带动精准扶贫项目实施。

五、高速铁路让流动的中国更具繁荣发展的活力

高速铁路串起“快”的中国，四通八达的高铁网络以更快的速度赋能人流、物流、资金流、信息流等一切生产要素，人们的联系更加紧密了，整个社会的运行效率更高了，产生了高铁“乘数效应”。有人说，高铁改变了中国经济版图；有人说，高铁改变了生活方式；有人说，高铁改变了思想观念……高铁给中国经济社会发展带来的影响是全

promoted the implementation of targeted poverty alleviation projects.

5 Making China More Prosperous and Vigorous

High-speed railway makes us fast, and the HSR network in all directions has enabled all factors of production such as human flow, logistics, capital flow and information flow at a faster speed. People are more closely connected, and the operation efficiency of the whole society is higher, resulting in the “multiplier effect” of HSR. Some people say that high-speed railway has changed the territory of China’s economy; some say that high-speed railway has changed the way of life; some say that high-speed railway has changed ideas... The impact of HSR on China’s economic and social development is comprehensive.

HSR saves social time cost and brings huge social time benefit. For

⊙正在飞驰的广深港高铁动感号列车
Guangzhou-Shenzhen-Hong Kong High-Speed Railway

方位的。

高速铁路节约社会时间成本，带来了巨大社会时间效益。如京广高铁武广段开通后，武汉到广州的列车运行时间由11小时缩短至4小时内。依据现阶段运量和单位时间劳动力成本测算，这条线路每年节约的社会时间成本价值数十亿元。

example, after the opening of Wuhan-Guangzhou section of Beijing-Guangzhou high-speed railway, the running time from Wuhan to Guangzhou has been shortened from 11 hours to 4 hours. According to the current traffic volume and unit time labour cost, the social time cost saved by this line is worth billions RMB every year.

The opening of high-speed railway releases the capacity of the existing line, and the turnover of people and logistics

高速铁路开通释放了既有线的运能，全社会人流、物流周转明显加快，成本降低。专家分析，在全社会货运量中，提高铁路运输比重将大大节约社会物流成本。

高速铁路的建设和运营，带动了冶金、机械、建筑、橡胶、电力、信息、精密仪器等产业的快速发展，为推动产业结构优化升级发挥了重要作用。据不完全统计，中国动车组零部件生产设计核心层企业140余家、紧密层企业500余家，覆盖20多个省市，形成了一个庞大的高新技术研发制造产业链。

in the whole society is obviously accelerated, and the cost is reduced. The analysis shows that, increasing the proportion of railway transportation will greatly save the cost of social logistics.

The construction and operation of HSR has led to the rapid development of metallurgy, machinery, construction, rubber, power, information, precision instruments and other industries, and has played an important role in promoting the optimization and upgrading of industrial structure. According to incomplete statistics, there are more than 140 core enterprises and 500 close-layer enterprises in China's EMU parts production and design, covering more than 20 provinces and cities, which formed a huge high-tech R&D and manufacturing industry chain.

第 6 章 走向未来的中国高速铁路

Chapter 6 High-Speed Railway into the Future

面向未来，中国铁路进一步推进铁路规划建设，大力推动高速铁路技术创新，不断续写创新发展新篇章。

Back to the future, China Railway has further promoted the implementation of railway construction planning, vigorously promoted technological innovation and continued to write a new chapter of innovation and development.

一、中国高速铁路发展规划

中国将加快建设以“八纵八横”主通道为骨架、区域连接线衔接、城际铁路补充的高速铁路网。到2020年，基本建成布局合理、覆盖广泛、高效便捷、功能完善、世界上最现代化的高速铁路网，高铁营业里程达到3万公里以上，覆盖中国80%以上的大城市；到2025年，高铁营业里程达到3.8万公里左右；到2035年，率先建成发达完善的现代化铁路网，基本实现内外互联互通、区际多路畅通、省会高铁连通、地市快速通达、县域基本覆盖，形成以特大城市为中心覆盖全国、以省会城市为支点覆盖周边的高

1 HSR Development Plan

China will speed up the development of its HSR network where the eight horizontal and eight vertical national railway network serves as the backbones, complemented by regional transfer lines and inter-city railway lines. By 2020, the country will have put in place the most advanced HSR network, featuring well-designed layout, extensive coverage, high efficiency, great convenience, and integrated performance. The operational mileage of HSR will be more than 30,000 km, covering over 80% of the country's major cities. By 2025, the number is expected to rise to around 38,000km. By 2035, the country will take the lead in building an advanced and comprehensive railway network that ensures interoperability, smooth regional access via multiple routes, HSR access to every provincial capital, rapid access to prefecture cities and a general coverage of all county regions. By then,

速铁路网，实现相邻大中城市间1至4小时交通圈，城市群内0.5至2小时交通圈，为基本实现社会主义现代化提供强大运输保障。

a HSR network—where big cities work as centres to provide nationwide coverage, while provincial capitals serve as pivots to include adjacent areas—will take shape, and the travelling time among neighbouring medium and big cities will be shortened to 1–4h, while that within the city clusters will be cut to 0.5–2h. Such a network will secure strong transport capacity while the nation is moving toward basically realizing socialist modernization.

⊙北京至张家口高速铁路官厅水库特大桥
Beijing-Zhangjiakou High-Speed Railway Line at GUANTING Reservoir Grand Bridge

⊙京雄城际雄安站效果图
The Effect Picture of Xiong'an Railway Station

二、智能高速铁路

采用云计算、大数据、物联网、移动互联、人工智能、BIM等先进技术与高速铁路的集成融合，实现高铁移动装备、固定基础设施及内外部环境间信息的全面感知、泛在互联、融合处理、

2 Intelligent High-Speed Railway

The integration of advanced technologies such as cloud computing, big data, Internet of Things, mobile interconnection, artificial intelligence , building information modeling with high-speed railway can makes full sensing of infor-

主动学习和科学决策，打造更加安全可靠、更加经济高效、更加方便快捷、更加绿色环保的新一代高速铁路系统，实现旅客智能出行、高铁智能运输，全面提升高铁安全生产、运营管理、客运服务的现代化水平。

mation possible, so it becomes ubiquitous and interconnected, and enables fusion processing, automated learning and scientific decision-making between high-speed railway mobile equipment, fixed infrastructure and internal and external environment. A new generation of high-speed railway system, which is more economical, efficient, convenient, green and environmental friendly, provides intelligent traveling services to passengers and enables intelligent transportation by HSRs, improving in an all-round way the modernization of safe production, operation, management and service of China's HSR network.

⊙智能高速铁路概念动车组
Creative Design Results of Intelligent EMU

⊙高速机车车辆及动车整车试验室

High-Speed Locomotive and Motor Vehicle Laboratory

⊙国家铁道试验中心环行线

Circular Line of Railway Test Center

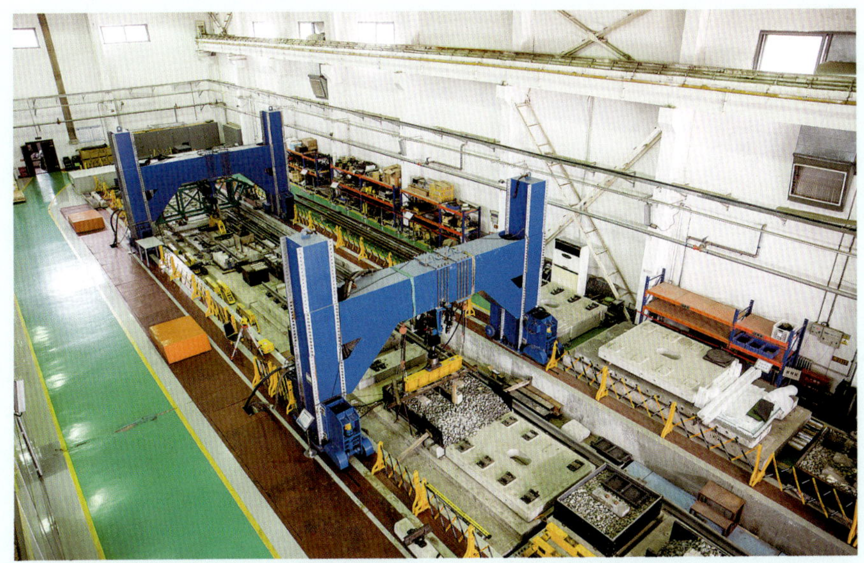

⊙高速铁路轨道技术国家重点实验室
The State Key Laboratory for High-Speed Railway Track Technology

⊙高速铁路弓网关系实验室
Pantograph-Gate Laboratory of High-Speed Railway

三、绿色高速铁路

充分发挥高速铁路在绿色交通体系建设中的比较优势，把绿色发展理念贯穿到高速铁路发展全过程，以高速铁路建设和运营为重点，以清洁低碳、集约高效、生态友好为主要目标，广泛应用先进的绿色技术，努力建设与自然资源承载力相匹配、与铁路沿线生态环境相协调的绿色高铁，实现高速铁路绿色发展、循环发展和可持续发展。

⊙复兴号飞驰广西秀丽山川
Fuxing EMUs Speeding on Picturesque Mountains and Beautiful Rivers of Guangxi

3 Green High-Speed Railway

Give full play to the comparative advantages of high-speed railway in the construction of green transportation system. Run the concept of green development throughout the whole process of high-speed railway development. Focus on the construction and operation of high-speed railway, in order to take clean, low-carbon, intensive, efficient and eco-friendly as the main objectives, widely apply advanced green technology. Strive to build the Green HSR, which matches the carrying capacity of the source and coordinates with the ecological environment along the railway, so as to achieve the green development, cyclic development and sustainable development.

四、与世界分享中国高速铁路发展经验

中国铁路围绕服务“一带一路”建设，坚持开放共享、合作共赢的原则，积极开展国际铁路合作。目前，印尼雅万高铁逐步进入全面施工阶段。中老铁路稳步推进，廉洁之路建

4. Sharing HSR Experiences with the Rest of the World

CHINA RAILWAY sticks to the principles of opening up, sharing and win-win cooperation, and actively carries out international cooperation. Indonesia Djakarta-Bandung HSR has gradually entered the stage of full construction. China-Laos Railway has steadily advanced and has achieved initial results. The first phase of China-Thai-

⊙印尼雅万高速铁路瓦利尼隧道
Varigny Tunnel of Djakarta-Bandung HSR in Indonesia

设初见成效。中泰铁路一期工程、巴基斯坦拉合尔橙线轻轨工程进展顺利。匈塞铁路塞尔维亚境内段开工建设，莫喀高铁前期工作有序推进。中国愿与世界各国加强交流合作，分享中国高速铁路发展经验，共创更加美好的明天。

land Railway and Pakistan Lahore Orange Line Light Rail are progressing smoothly. Construction of the Hungarian-Serbian Railway has started in Serbia, and the early stage work of the Mokha High-speed Railway has been carried out in an orderly manner. China is willing to enhance exchange and cooperation with all countries, share China's know-how on HSR development and work together for a brighter future.

⊙中老铁路磨丁隧道出口
Boten Tunnel Exit along the China-Laos Railway

◎ 中老铁路万象段路基工程
Vientiane Subgrade Engineering of China-Laos Railway

⊙巴基斯坦拉合尔橙线轻轨铁路
Pakistan Lahore Orange Line Light Rail

⊙中老铁路琅勃拉邦跨湄公河特大桥
China-Laos railway's Luang Prabang Bridge over Mekong River

⊙雅万高铁1号隧道的盾构机施工
Shield in Construction of No.1 Tunnel of Djakarta-Bandung HSR in Indonesia

⊙匈塞铁路塞尔维亚境内段开工
Construction of the Hungarian-Serbian Railway Started in Serbian

图书在版编目（CIP）数据

快速发展的中国高速铁路 --The Rapid Development of China's High-speed Railways ：汉英对照 / 中国国家铁路集团有限公司编. -- 北京 ：中国铁道出版社有限公司，2019.9（2019.11重印）

ISBN 978-7-113-25660-9

Ⅰ. ①快… Ⅱ. ①中… Ⅲ. ①高速铁路－铁路运输发展－中国－汉、英 Ⅳ. ①F532.3

中国版本图书馆CIP数据核字(2019)第054347号

书　　名：**快速发展的中国高速铁路**
The Rapid Development of China's High-Speed Railways

作　　者：中国国家铁路集团有限公司
CHINA STATE RAILWAY GROUP CO., LTD.

责任编辑：曾亚非　郭力伟

书籍设计：德浩设计工作室

封面设计：崔　欣

摄　　影：史家民、原瑞伦、杨宝森、罗春晓、陈涛、王明柱、伍光钦、丁波、彭琦、赵萌等

责任印制：赵星辰

出版发行：中国铁道出版社有限公司（100054，北京市西城区右安门西街8号）

网　　址：http://www.tdpress.com

印　　制：中煤（北京）印务有限公司

版　　次：2019 年9月第 1 版　2019 年11月第 2 次印刷

开　　本：700mm× 1000mm　1/16　印张：9.25　字数：20 千

书　　号：ISBN 978-7-113-25660-9

定　　价：48.00 元